10-06

PREHISTORIC CREATURES IN THE SEA & SKY

Brenda Ralph Lewis

GARETH**STEVENS**
PUBLISHING
A Member of the WRC Media Family of Companies

Please visit our Web site at: **www.garethstevens.com**
For a free color catalog describing Gareth Stevens Publishing's
list of high-quality books and multimedia programs,
call 1-800-542-2595 (USA) or 1-800-387-3178 (Canada).
Gareth Stevens Publishing's fax: (414) 332-3567.

Library of Congress Cataloging-in-Publication Data

Lewis, Brenda Ralph.
    Prehistoric creatures in the sea & sky / Brenda Ralph Lewis.
        p. cm. — (Nature's monsters. Dinosaurs)
    Includes bibliographical references and index.
    ISBN-10: 0-8368-6845-5 — ISBN-13: 978-0-8368-6845-6 (lib. bdg.)
    1. Animals, Fossil—Juvenile literature.   2. Marine animals, Fossil—Juvenile literature.
    I. Title. II. Series.
    QE842.L49   2006
    567.9—dc22   20060042362

This North American edition first published in 2007 by
Gareth Stevens Publishing
A Member of the WRC Media Family of Companies
330 West Olive Street, Suite 100
Milwaukee, WI 53212 USA

Original edition and illustrations copyright © 2006 by International Masters Publishers AB.
Produced by Amber Books Ltd., Bradley's Close, 74–77 White Lion Street, London N1 9PF, U.K.

Project editor: Michael Spilling
Design: Graham Curd

Gareth Stevens editorial direction: Valerie J. Weber
Gareth Stevens editor: Leifa Butrick
Gareth Stevens art direction: Tammy West
Gareth Stevens production: Jessica Morris

Printed in the United States of America

1 2 3 4 5 6 7 8 9 10 09 08 07 06

Contents

Continents of the World

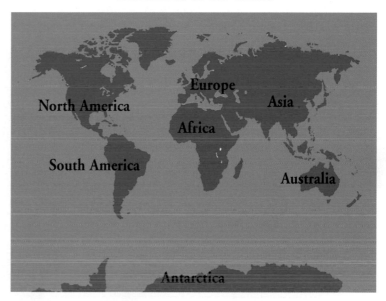

The world is divided into seven continents —
North America, South America, Europe, Africa,
Asia, Australia, and Antarctica. On the following
pages, the area where each dinosaur was
discovered is shown in red, while all land
is shown in green.

Words that appear in the glossary are printed in
boldface type the first time they occur in the text.

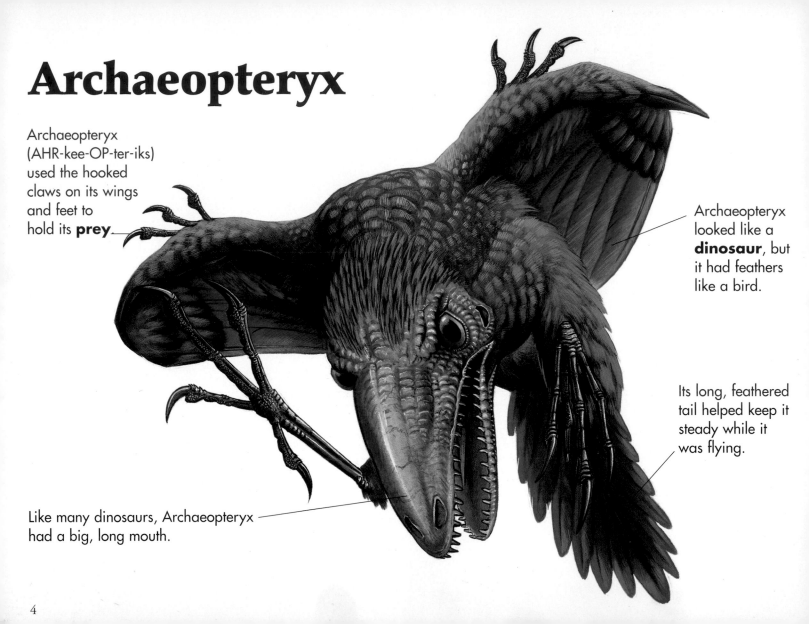

Archaeopteryx

Archaeopteryx (AHR-kee-OP-ter-iks) used the hooked claws on its wings and feet to hold its **prey.**

Archaeopteryx looked like a **dinosaur**, but it had feathers like a bird.

Its long, feathered tail helped keep it steady while it was flying.

Like many dinosaurs, Archaeopteryx had a big, long mouth.

Archaeopteryx had the teeth, claws, and tail of a killer dinosaur, but it was also feathered and had wings, like a bird today. It lived in open forest.

Size

1 Like a bird, Archaeopteryx had to learn how to fly. One way was to use its **talons** to climb a tree and then jump off a branch, throwing itself into the air. By spreading out its wings and its tail, it could **glide** for a short distance.

2 Another way was to stand on the ground and keep on jumping higher and higher. After a while, Archaeopteryx could stay in the air long enough to flap its wings and start flying.

Where in the World

Archaeopteryx was about 13 inches (33 centimeters) long. Seven **fossils** were found preserved in limestone in Bavaria, southern Germany, where the bird lived in late **Jurassic** times (about 150 million years ago).

Coelurosauravus

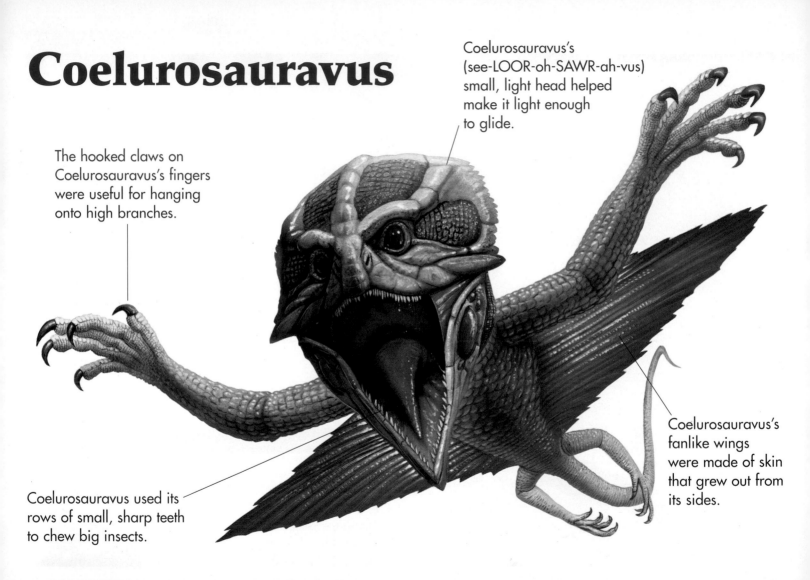

Coelurosauravus's (see-LOOR-oh-SAWR-ah-vus) small, light head helped make it light enough to glide.

The hooked claws on Coelurosauravus's fingers were useful for hanging onto high branches.

Coelurosauravus used its rows of small, sharp teeth to chew big insects.

Coelurosauravus's fanlike wings were made of skin that grew out from its sides.

Coelurosauravus had bony rods in its wings. For this reason, some **paleontologists** called it the first flying reptile. Its stretched-out flaps of skin were not real wings, however — they could not be flapped and could only be used for gliding.

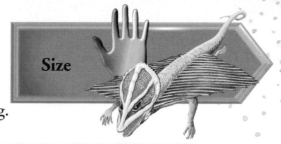

Size

1 Because Coelurosuaravus was **cold-blooded**, it needed to warm up its body every morning. Here, some of these ancient flying lizards use their hooked fingers to hang from big **conifers**, spreading their wings to soak up heat from the Sun.

2 When shadows fall across the conifers, the Coelurosuaravus leaps a short distance to glide to another tree that still stands in the sunlight.

Where in the World

Coelurosauravus fossils were first found in England in 1910. Others were discovered on Madagascar, off eastern Africa, and in Germany. Coelurosauravus lived in early Triassic times.

Deinosuchus

Deinosuchus's (die-no-SUE-kus) jaw was 6 feet (1.8 meters) long and contained one hundred teeth.

Bony plates covered with thick scales protected it from attack by other dinosaurs.

Deinosuchus swam through the water by moving its tail from side to side.

Deinosuchus could open its mouth very wide by using long, powerful muscles.

8

At 49 feet (15 meters) long, Deinosuchus was the largest crocodile that ever lived. Deinosuchus hunted its prey in swamps, marshes, and rivers. It had an enormous appetite and needed huge meals.

Deinosuchus weighed about 5 tons (4.5 metric tons). It swallowed stones so that it could sink below the water's surface to wait for the large animals it killed and ate.

1 A Deinosuchus swims in the shallow waters of the wetlands. It waits for prey to come to the water's edge. Its prey is unaware that this **predator** is hiding in the shallows.

2 Without warning, the Deinosuchus leaps up. Its massive jaws close around its prey's neck. It pushes its prey under the water, where the animal drowns. Soon the Deinosuchus is tearing chunks of flesh from its body.

Where in the World

Deinosuchus lived during the **Cretaceous** period, from 144 to 65 million years ago. Its **habitat** in North America was covered by swamps, marshes, and shallow waters.

Dimorphodon

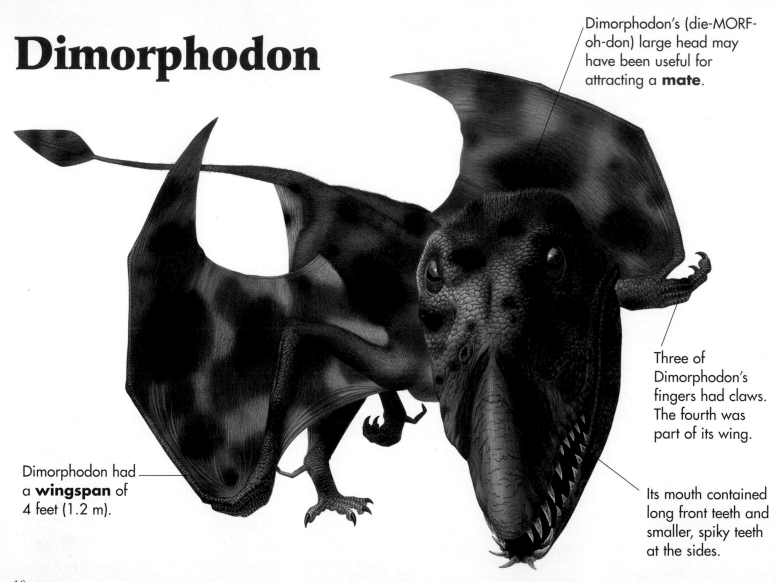

Dimorphodon's (die-MORF-oh-don) large head may have been useful for attracting a **mate**.

Three of Dimorphodon's fingers had claws. The fourth was part of its wing.

Dimorphodon had a **wingspan** of 4 feet (1.2 m).

Its mouth contained long front teeth and smaller, spiky teeth at the sides.

Dimorphodon was a carnivore. As a flying creature, it often covered long distances hunting for food. Dimorphodon had very good eyesight and could see its prey from a long way off.

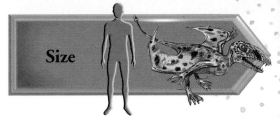

Size

Did You Know?

The Dimorphodon was not a dinosaur, it was a **pterosaur** (TER-uh-sawr). Ptereosaurs were flying reptiles, not **prehistoric** birds, like Archaeopteryx.

1 A lizard lies **basking** on a rock, enjoying the warm Sun. A Dimorphodon spots the lizard and flies down toward it. The lizard sees the Dimorphodon approaching and starts to run way.

2 The Dimorphodon swoops down, seizes the lizard's neck in its jaws, and kills the lizard with one bite. The Dimorphodon bites off big chunks of the lizard's flesh with its small, spiky teeth. Afterward, it uses its long, knifelike front teeth to slice up the meat into smaller pieces.

Where in the World

Dimorphodon lived in southwestern England and Mexico in the early Jurassic period, 206 million years ago. Today, these two places are far apart. They were both part of a huge continent known as Pangea when the Dimorphodons lived.

Dunkleosteus

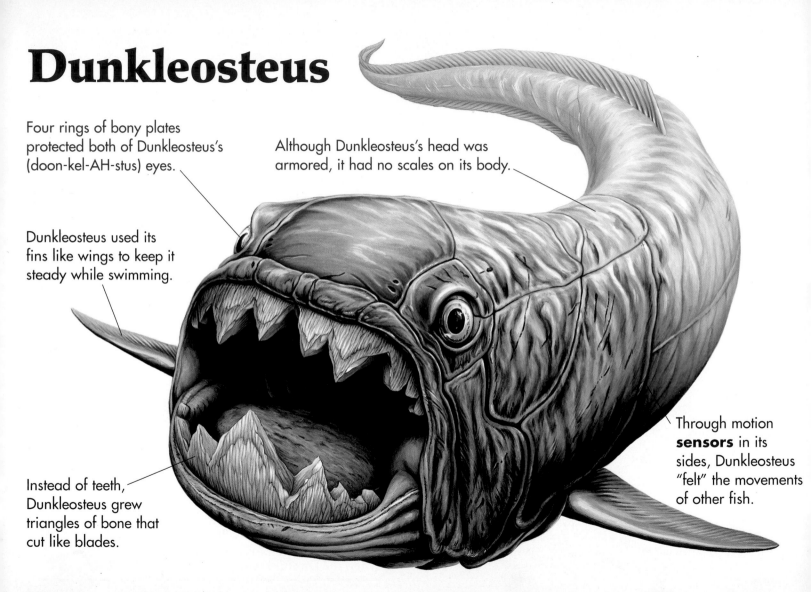

Four rings of bony plates protected both of Dunkleosteus's (doon-kel-AH-stus) eyes.

Although Dunkleosteus's head was armored, it had no scales on its body.

Dunkleosteus used its fins like wings to keep it steady while swimming.

Instead of teeth, Dunkleosteus grew triangles of bone that cut like blades.

Through motion **sensors** in its sides, Dunkleosteus "felt" the movements of other fish.

Dunkleosteus was not a shark. It was a placoderm — an armored fish with a jaw. It had a tail like a shark's, and like a shark, it was a terrifying predator.

1 A Dunkleosteus's motion sensors pick up a nearby Holocephalan — a small, bony fish. The Holocephalan has no chance of escaping. The Dunkleosteus comes closer, sees the little fish, and attacks.

Size

2 With one bite of its enormous jaws, the Dunkleosteus bites the Holocephalan in half. It swallows the tail first, then eats the rest.

Where in the World

Fossil bones of Dunkleosteus have been found in eastern North America, Morocco, Germany, Poland, and Belgium. They lived in the late **Devonian** period, about 360 million years ago.

Hesperornis

Hesperornis (HES-per-OR-nis) could see well under water. Its eyesight was not as good on land.

Hesperornis's slim body was perfect for diving and moving fast through water.

With webbed feet like a duck's, Hesperornis was a powerful swimmer.

Hesperornis's long, slim bill helped it catch many fish at one time.

Life on land could be dangerous for Hesperornis. It moved too slowly to escape predators. It was much safer in the sea, where it probably spent most of its time.

Size

Did You Know?

Although Hesperornis had short wings, it could not fly. It used the sharp claws on its feet to cling to rocks before diving into the sea to catch its prey.

1 A Hesperornis is paddling along in the sea, looking for fish or squid to catch and eat. A big Pteranodon, a flying reptile, soars overhead. It, too, is looking for fish to eat.

2 The Hesperornis sees a squid before the Pteranodon can pounce. It dives deep down in the water. Kicking its webbed feet for speed, it catches up with the squid. The Hesperornis seizes its prey and moves up to the surface, where it swallows the squid in one gulp.

Fossil bones of Hesperornis have often been found between Kansas and northern Canada. Hesperornis lived in this part of North America during the Cretaceous period, from 144 to 65 million years ago.

Kronosaurus

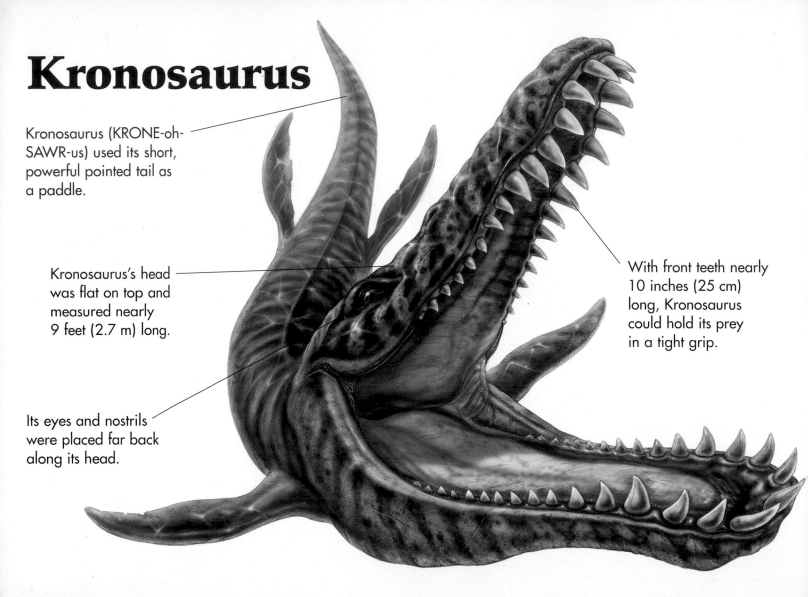

Kronosaurus (KRONE-oh-SAWR-us) used its short, powerful pointed tail as a paddle.

Kronosaurus's head was flat on top and measured nearly 9 feet (2.7 m) long.

Its eyes and nostrils were placed far back along its head.

With front teeth nearly 10 inches (25 cm) long, Kronosaurus could hold its prey in a tight grip.

Using fossils, paleontologists have been able to tell what Kronosaurus looked like and what it ate. They do not know yet how a mother Kronosaurus gave birth to her young.

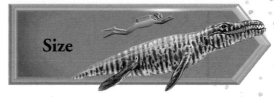

In 1932, some Kronosaurus fossils were discovered in rock and blasted out using dynamite. Experts used these fossils to make a model of Kronosaurus. The fossil bones were not complete, however, so scientists used **plaster of paris** to fill in the gaps.

1 One **theory** is that the female Kronosaurus dug a hole in a sandy beach with her flippers. After laying her eggs in the hole, she covered them up with sand and returned to the sea. After **hatching** from the eggs, the babies were in danger from predators, which could kill and eat them.

2 Another idea sounds like a safer way to give birth. Some paleontologists think that baby Kronosaurus hatched inside their mother's body. Later, they were born in the sea.

Where in the World

Kronosaurus lived during the Cretaceous period, from 144 to 65 million years ago. Fossils were found in Queensland, Australia, as early as 1899.

17

Libonectes

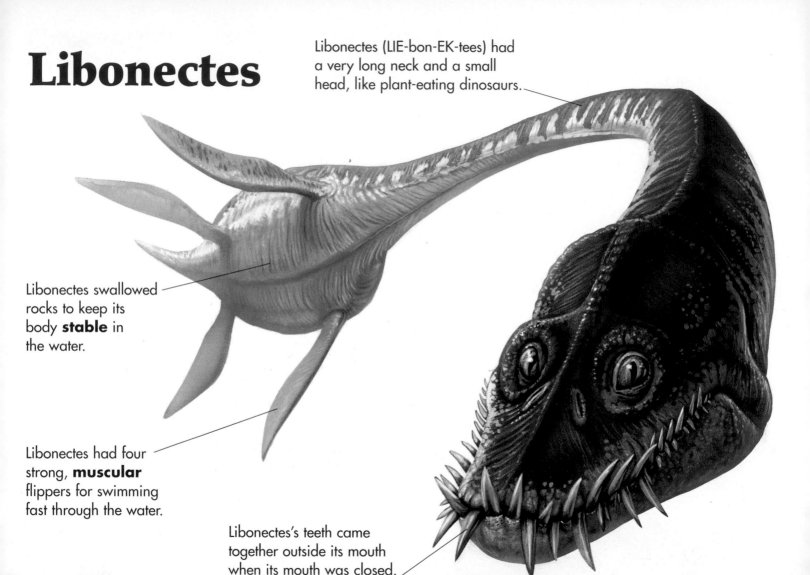

Libonectes (LIE-bon-EK-tees) had a very long neck and a small head, like plant-eating dinosaurs.

Libonectes swallowed rocks to keep its body **stable** in the water.

Libonectes had four strong, **muscular** flippers for swimming fast through the water.

Libonectes's teeth came together outside its mouth when its mouth was closed.

Reconstructing prehistoric animals from fossils is like doing a jigsaw puzzle with a lot of pieces missing. Without all the pieces, paleontologists can make mistakes.

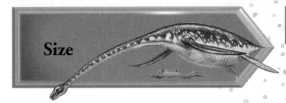

Size

Did You Know?

Libonectes had thirty-six teeth and sixty-two bones in its neck. Its neck made up nearly half of its body length, which was about 45 feet (14 m) long.

1 Paleontologists once believed that Libonectes caught its food by lifting its head high above the water and bringing it down hard on fish and squid swimming on the surface, stunning the prey.

2 Now they believe it was impossible for Libonectes to use its head in that way. The base of its neck was too stiff, and its neck only moved easily from side to side. Libonectes probably chased groups of fish and turned its head quickly to catch as many of them in its mouth as it could.

Where in the World

Libonectes lived during the Cretaceous period from 144 to 65 million years ago. It swam in the seas that covered what are now the states of Texas and Kansas.

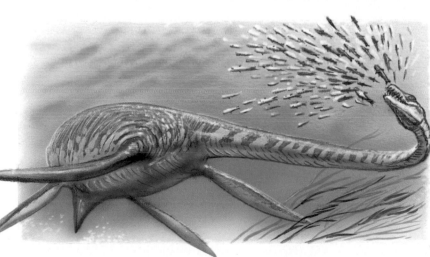

Mosasaur

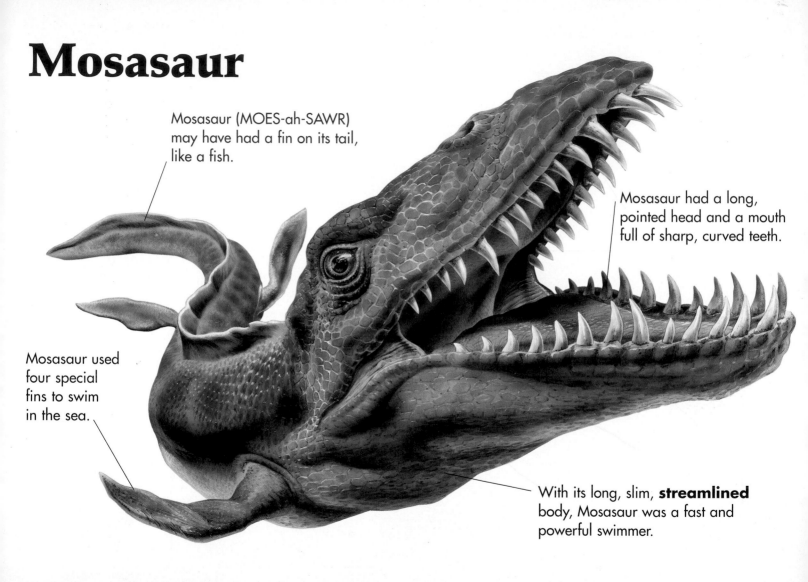

Mosasaur (MOES-ah-SAWR) may have had a fin on its tail, like a fish.

Mosasaur had a long, pointed head and a mouth full of sharp, curved teeth.

Mosasaur used four special fins to swim in the sea.

With its long, slim, **streamlined** body, Mosasaur was a fast and powerful swimmer.

With massive jaws lined with sharp teeth, Mosasaurs were the deadliest sea predators of their time. They preyed on fish, squid, and even smaller mosasaurs.

Size

1 Up to 95 million years ago, Ichthyosaurs, or "fish lizards," were the most common **marine** reptiles on Earth. They were fierce and speedy and, like Mosasaurs, lived on fish and squid.

2 After Ichthyosaurs started to die out, Mosasaurs competed for their food with Pliosaurs — the biggest carnivores that lived in the seas in the Jurassic period.

3 About 85 million years ago, the Mosasaurs became the most successful predator in the shallow seas where they lived.

Where in the World

Mosasaurs, which lived during the Cretaceous period (144 to 65 million years ago), left fossils all over the world, from Europe to North and South America, and from Africa to Australia.

Ophthalmosaurus

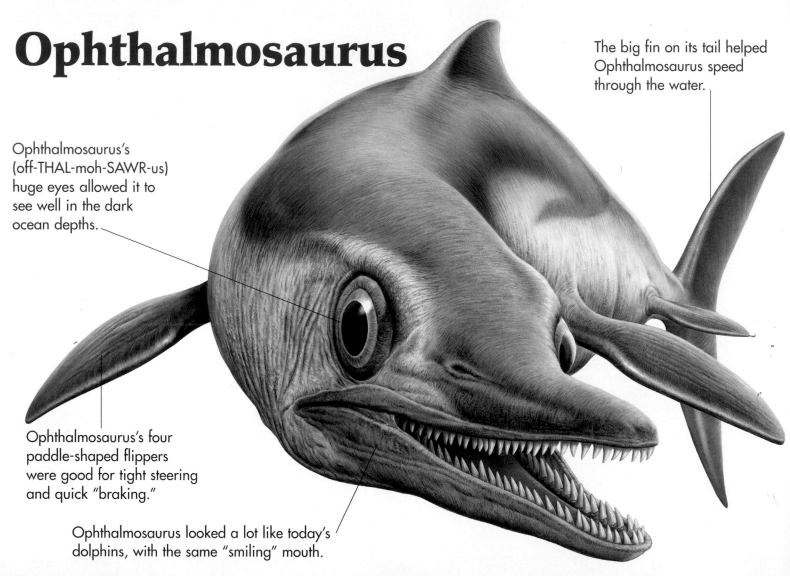

The big fin on its tail helped Ophthalmosaurus speed through the water.

Ophthalmosaurus's (off-THAL-moh-SAWR-us) huge eyes allowed it to see well in the dark ocean depths.

Ophthalmosaurus's four paddle-shaped flippers were good for tight steering and quick "braking."

Ophthalmosaurus looked a lot like today's dolphins, with the same "smiling" mouth.

It is difficult to find complete fossils of prehistoric creatures. Paleontologists have found complete Ophthalmosaurus fossils, however. They have learned a lot about Ophthalmosaurus from these fossils, including the way they gave birth.

Size

1 A female Ophthalmosaurus is ready to give birth to her baby, but she is in trouble. The baby is trapped in her **birth canal**. The mother is losing blood and growing weaker and weaker.

2 At last, she has no strength left and dies. Her body drifts down to the ocean bed. Sadly, her unborn baby dies with her.

3 Millions of years later, paleontologists find the skeletons of the mother and baby. After such a long time, their bodies have become fossils.

Where in the World

Ophthalmosaurus lived all over the world during the Jurassic period, from 208 to 144 million years ago. The first fossils were found in England in the early 1700s.

Pteranodon

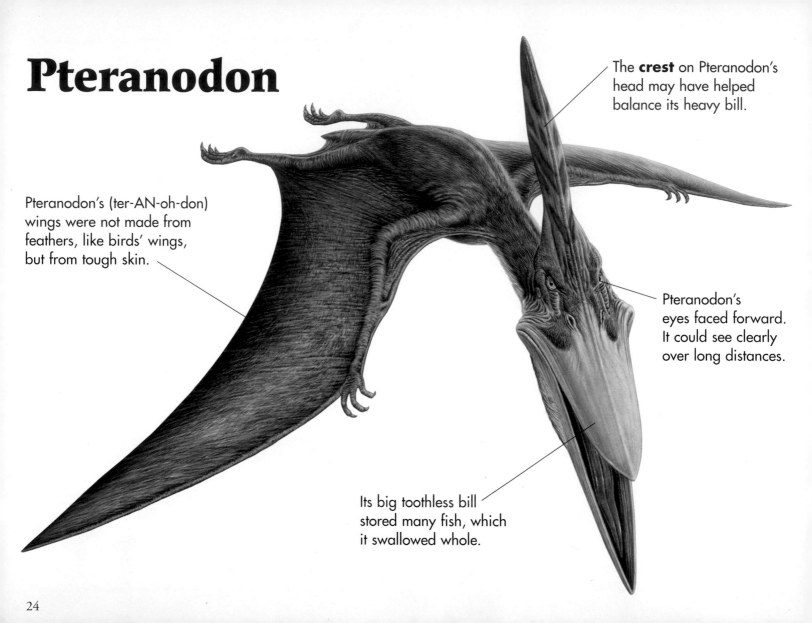

The **crest** on Pteranodon's head may have helped balance its heavy bill.

Pteranodon's (ter-AN-oh-don) wings were not made from feathers, like birds' wings, but from tough skin.

Pteranodon's eyes faced forward. It could see clearly over long distances.

Its big toothless bill stored many fish, which it swallowed whole.

Pteranodon was part of a family of prehistoric creatures called pterosaurs, which means "flying reptiles." Pterosaurs came in many shapes and sizes. Eudimorphodon (YOO-dih-MORF-oh-don), for example, was small — only the size of today's gulls. Next to Eudimorphodon, Pteranodon was a giant.

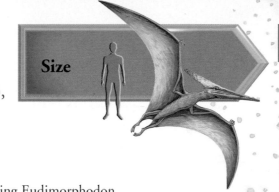

Size

Did You Know?

Pteranodon's 33-foot (10-m) wingspan was larger than the wingspan of any bird today. Standing about 6 feet (1.8 m) tall, Pteranodon weighed around 44 pounds (20 kilograms).

1 The fish-eating Eudimorphodon had a long neck, a large head, and pointed jaws. It was one of the first flying reptiles.

2 Pterodaustro, another pterosaur, looked as if it had a brush in its mouth. It squeezed a mouthful of water through its five hundred bristles, leaving tiny animals behind to eat.

3 Like Pterodaustro, Pteranodon's bill curved upward. Pteranodon may have used the sharp sides of its bill to cut up large fish that it could not swallow whole.

Where in the World

During the Cretaceous period from 144 to 65 million years ago, Pteranodon lived by the sea that then covered Kansas. The first Pteranodon fossils were found in 1876 in Smoky Hill River, Kansas.

Pterodaustro

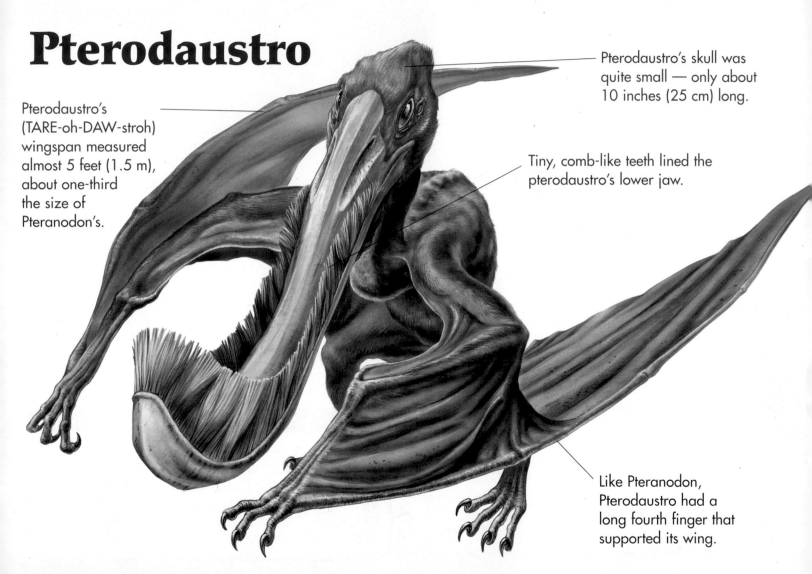

Pterodaustro's (TARE-oh-DAW-stroh) wingspan measured almost 5 feet (1.5 m), about one-third the size of Pteranodon's.

Pterodaustro's skull was quite small — only about 10 inches (25 cm) long.

Tiny, comb-like teeth lined the pterodaustro's lower jaw.

Like Pteranodon, Pterodaustro had a long fourth finger that supported its wing.

Pterodaustro spent a lot of its time gliding on outstretched wings high across the skies of prehistoric South America looking for food.

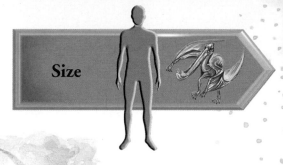

Thousands of tiny living creatures called **parasites** may have lived in the skin of Pterodaustro's wings. It probably took hours for a Pterodaustro to remove them so that it could fly properly.

1 Flying high above a lake, a Pterodaustro sees other pterosaurs feeding. The Pterodaustro swoops down and lands on the shore. In the water, it starts stamping its feet in the mud on the bed of the lake. The movements stir up the mud, which is full of tiny animals to eat.

2 The Pterodaustro bends down and scoops up a big mouthful of water. The water runs out the sides of its mouth, but the food stays inside.

Where in the World

Pterodaustro fossils were first found in Argentina in 1970. The pterosaur lived all over South America during the Cretaceous period from 144 to 65 million years ago.

Quetzalcoatlus

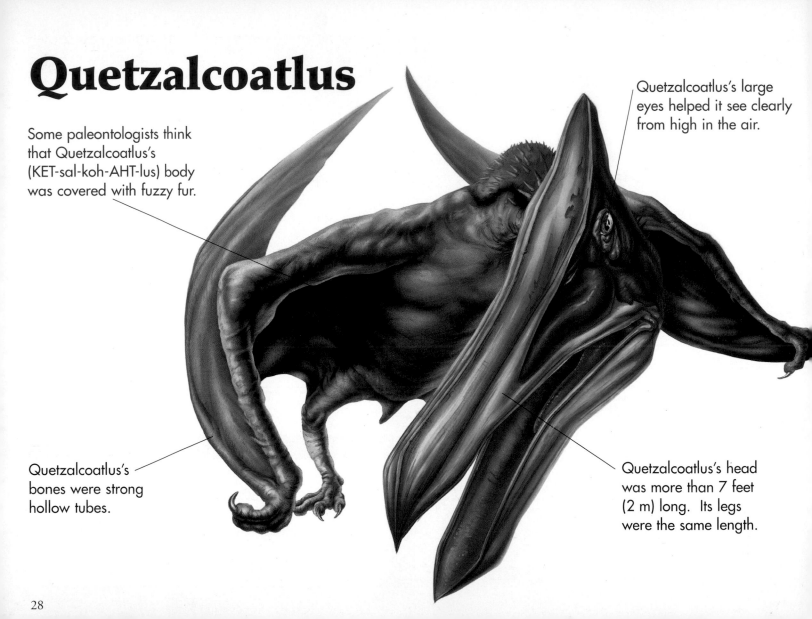

Some paleontologists think that Quetzalcoatlus's (KET-sal-koh-AHT-lus) body was covered with fuzzy fur.

Quetzalcoatlus's large eyes helped it see clearly from high in the air.

Quetzalcoatlus's bones were strong hollow tubes.

Quetzalcoatlus's head was more than 7 feet (2 m) long. Its legs were the same length.

Rising currents of hot air called thermals help birds, gliders, and balloons move upward into the sky. In prehistoric times, flying reptiles also "rode" thermals while flying through the air.

As a flying reptile, the Quetzalcoatlus may have been the biggest animal that ever flew. Quetzalcoatlus had an enormous wingspan, more than 39 feet (12 m) long.

1 A young Quetzalcoatlus leaps from the ground, eager to join other Quetzalcoatlus in the air. It must beat its wings about twenty times to move fast enough to reach the other reptiles flying overhead.

2 A column of warm air heated by the Sun rises from a nearby hill and lifts the young Quetzalcoatlus upward. The Quetzalcoatlus soon joins the other reptiles circling over pools in search of fish to eat.

Where in the World

During the Cretaceous period, from 144 to 65 million years ago, Quetzalcoatlus lived in Texas and in Canada. The first Quetzalcoatlus fossils were found in 1971 in Big Bend National Park, Texas.

29

Glossary

basking — lying in the warmth of the Sun

birth canal — a passage inside a mother through which a baby passes to be born

carnivore — a meat-eater

cold-blooded — having a body temperature that varies according to the animal's surroundings

conifers — trees whose leaves or needles do not drop

crest — a raised line or ridge of skin on an animal

Cretaceous — a period of time from 144 to 65 million years ago, when dinosaurs roamed Earth

Devonian — a period of time from 416 to 350 million years ago, before dinosaurs

dinosaur — various reptiles that lived on Earth from 245 to 65 million years ago but have since died out

extinct — no longer in existence

fossils — remains or imprints of animals and dinosaurs from an earlier time, often prehistoric; fossils are found beneath Earth's surface, pressed into rocks

glide — to travel through the air, floating on air currents without having to flap wings

habitat — a place where an animal or plant lives

hatching — breaking out of the shell of an egg

Jurassic — a period of time from 206 to 144 million years ago, when the first birds appeared

marine — referring to things that live in water

mate — a partner for making babies

muscular — having lots of muscle, the material that gives the body strength

paleontologists — scientists who study plant and animal life in prehistoric times (before human life began on Earth)

parasites — plants and animals that live on other plants and animals

plaster of paris — a soft paste that hardens when it dries

predator — an animal that hunts and kills other animals for food

prehistoric — the time before human history began

prey — an animal hunted for food

pterosaur — flying reptiles from the dinosaur age. They existed from the late Triassic to the end of the Cretaceous period (228 to 65 million years ago)

reconstructing — putting together again

sensors — parts of an animal that detect things, such as heat or movement

stable — steady and balanced

streamlined — designed to move through air or liquid as smoothly as possible

talons — sharp claws shaped like big hooks

theory — an idea put forward to explain something

Triassic — a period of time from 248 to 206 million years ago, when many reptiles, including dinosaurs, first appeared

wingspan — measurement of a flying creature's wings from the end of one wingtip to the end of the other

For More Information

Books

Dinosaurs. A Natural History. Paul Barrett (Simon & Schuster)

Feathered Dinosaurs. Meet the Dinosaurs (series). Don Lessem (Lerner Publications)

Monsters of the Sea. When Dinosaurs Lived (series). Don Lessem (Grosset & Dunlap)

National Geographic Dinosaurs. For the Junior Rockhound (series). Paul Barrett (National Geographic Children's Books)

Prehistoric Flying Reptiles: The Pterosaurs. Dinosaur Library (series). Thom Holmes and Laurie Holmes (Enslow Publishers)

True-Life Monsters of the Prehistoric Seas. World of Dinosaurs (series). Enid B. Fisher (Gareth Stevens Publishing)

Web Sites

Dinosaur Illustrations
www.search4dinosaurs.com

Dinosaurs Online
www.kidsturncentral.com/links/dinolinks.htm

Dinosaur Time Machine
www.mantyweb.com/dinosaur

Pterosaurs
members.aol.com/Dinoplanet/pter_gallery.html

Zoom Dinosaurs: EnchantedLearning.com
www.enchantedlearning.com/subjects/dinosaurs

Publisher's note to educators and parents: Our editors have carefully reviewed these Web sites to ensure that they are suitable for children. Many Web sites change frequently, however, and we cannot guarantee that a site's future contents will continue to meet our high standards of quality and educational value. Be advised that children should be closely supervised whenever they access the Internet.

Index